DINOJITSU

Guards & Passes

Brazilian Jiu-Jitsu Coloring Book

Monkey Mount

COLLECT THE WHOLE
DINOJITSU SERIES!

A word to grown-ups from Monkey Mount

Monkey Mount is a team of creatives and Jiu Jitsu practitioners with a common goal: *to inspire others*. This community was created by Brazilian Jiu-Jitsu and Judo Black Belt Yacinta Nguyen with the intent of inspiring her students to see the magic in the martial arts that have transformed her life.

Professor Yacinta Nguyen is among the elite Brazilian Jiu Jitsu practitioners in Canada. She holds accolades from the most prestigious competitions around the world and is also featured on the *BJJ Heroes* website. Moreover, her passion and focus now is to bring together the wonderful talent in the community and leverage Brazilian Jiu-Jitsu as a means to:

- empower our children through *confidence building* and *resilience training*
- show young girls that *strong is beautiful*
- improve *mental health* in the community

We hope you enjoy this coloring book as much as we enjoyed creating it. If you did, please consider taking a moment out of your busy day to leave us a review, this is more helpful than you can imagine and will allow us to keep on creating more books for the community.

With Love,

The Monkey Mount Team

 JOIN OUR COMMUNITY ON SOCIAL MEDIA!
@MONKEYMOUNTBOOKS

FIST BUMP

FIST BUMP

CLOSED GUARD

CLOSED GUARD

CLOSED GUARD

X PASS

X PASS

X PASS

50/50 GUARD

50/50 GUARD

LEG DRAG PASS

LEG DRAG PASS

BUTTERFLY GUARD

BUTTERFLY
GUARD

BUTTERFLY GUARD

LONG STEP PASS

LONG STEP PASS

K GUARD

K GUARD

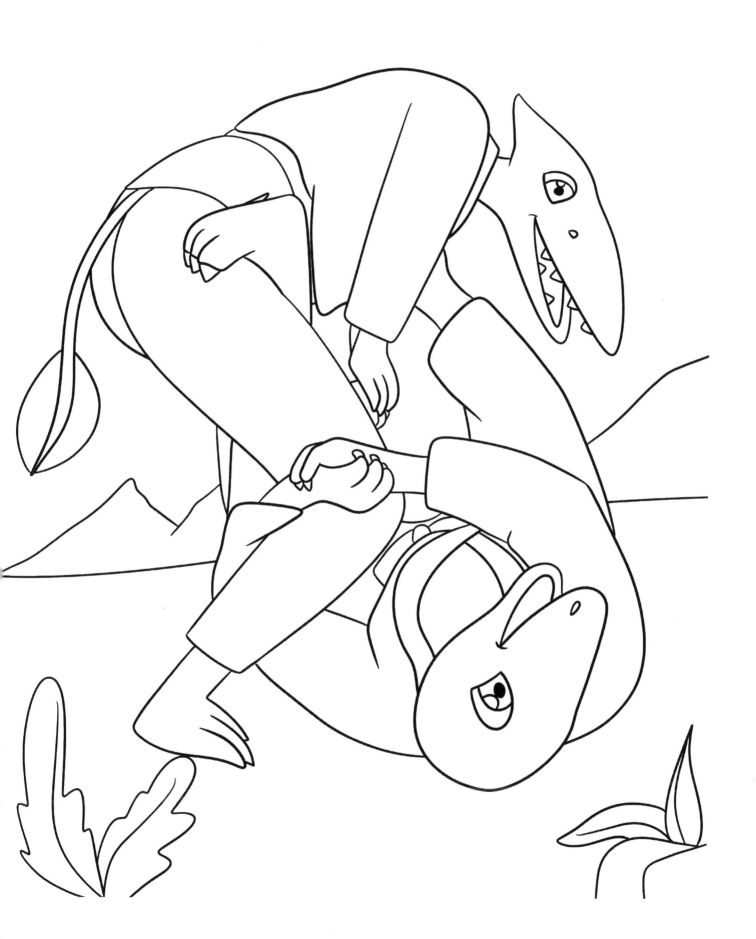

TOREANDO

TOREANDO

DE LA RIVA GUARD

DE LA RIVA GUARD

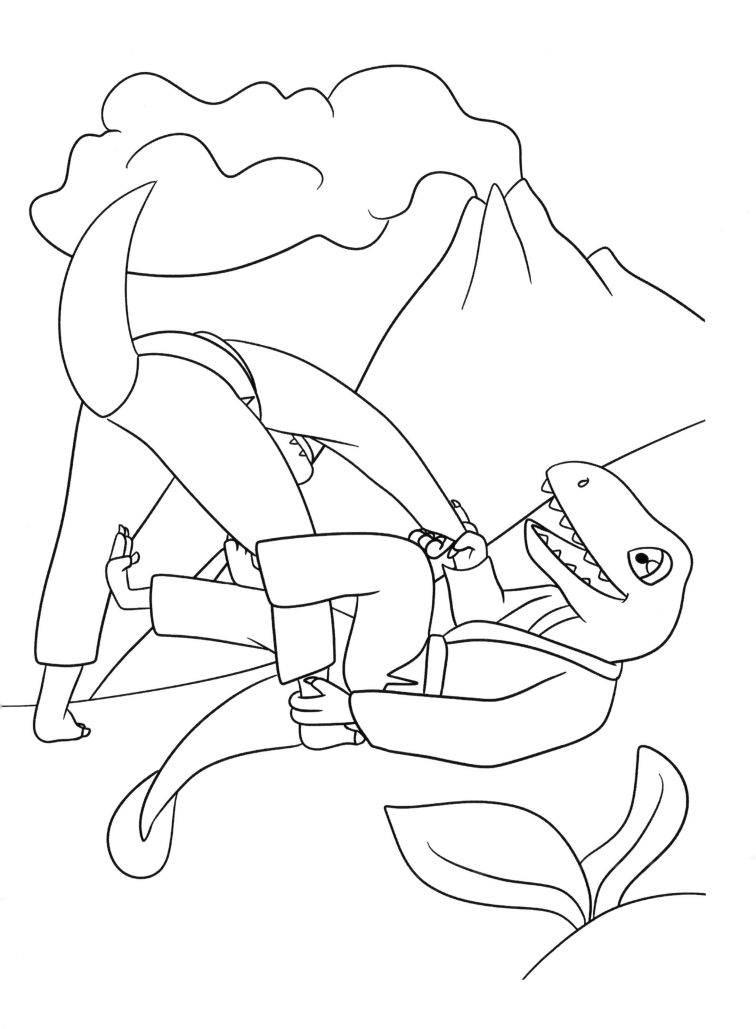

DOUBLE UNDER PASS

DOUBLE UNDER PASS

DOUBLE UNDER PASS

HALF GUARD

HALF GUARD

KNEE CUT PASS

KNEE CUT PASS

X GUARD

X GUARD

OVER UNDER PASS

OVER UNDER PASS

SPIDER GUARD

SPIDER GUARD

Made in the USA
Las Vegas, NV
09 December 2024

13733385R00039